LUDWIG VAN BEETHOVEN

SONATE

d-Moll / D minor

(»Sturmsonate / The Tempest«)

für Klavier / for Piano

op. 31 Nr. 2

Nach den Quellen herausgegeben von / Edited from the sources by

Johannes Fischer

EIGENTUM DES VERLEGERS · ALLE RECHTE VORBEHALTEN
ALL RIGHTS RESERVED

C. F. PETERS

FRANKFURT/M. · LEIPZIG · LONDON · NEW YORK

Largo – Allegro	1
Adagio	8
Allegretto	13
Kommentar / Commentary	24

SONATE

Ludwig van Beethoven (1770–1827)
op. 31 Nr. 2

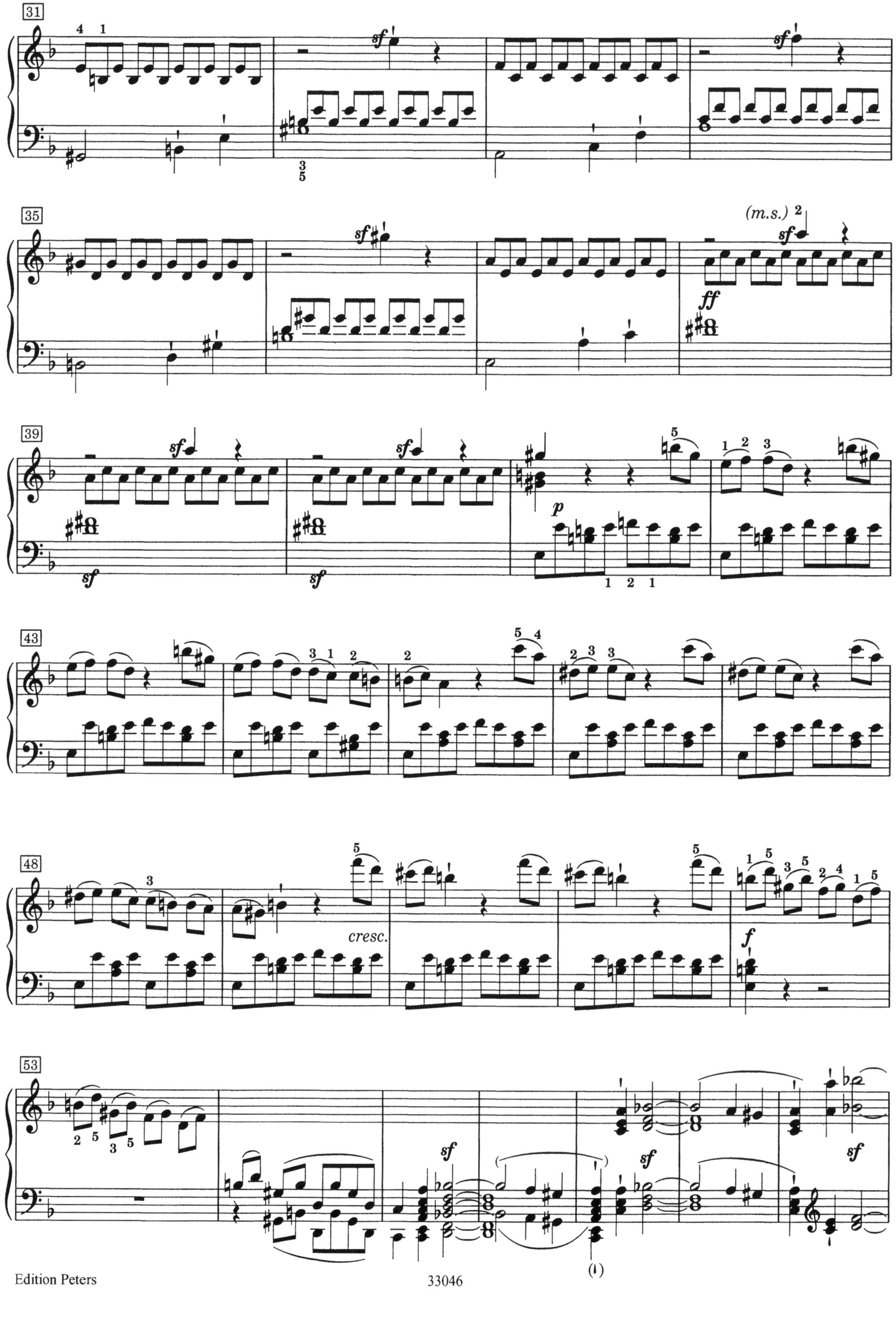
31
sf
35
sf
(m.s.)
sf
ff
39
sf
sf
sf
sf
p
43
48
cresc.
f
53
sf
sf
sf

*) Zur Ausführung siehe Revisionsbericht.

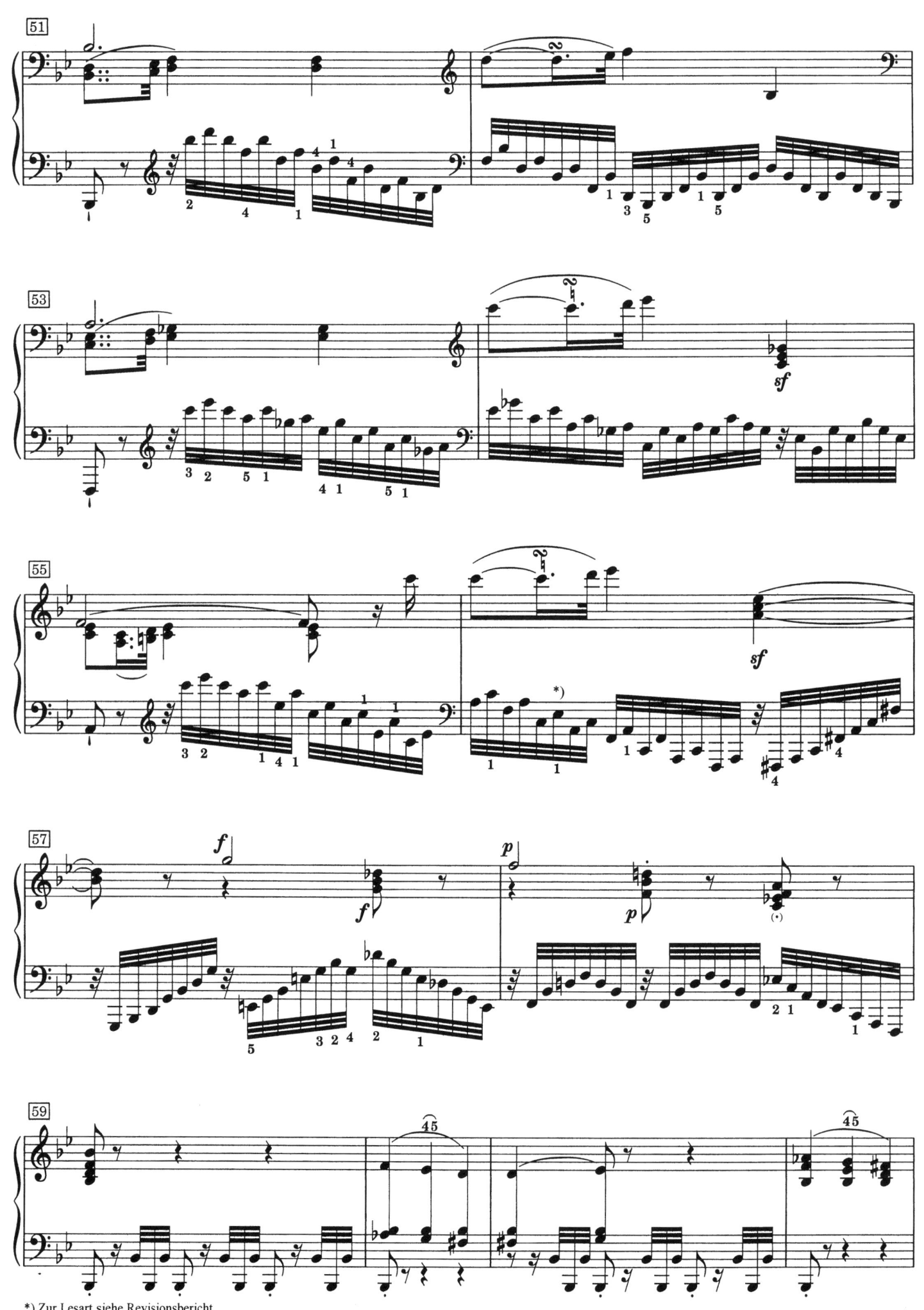

*) Zur Lesart siehe Revisionsbericht.
Edition Peters

*) Zur Lesart siehe Revisionsbericht.

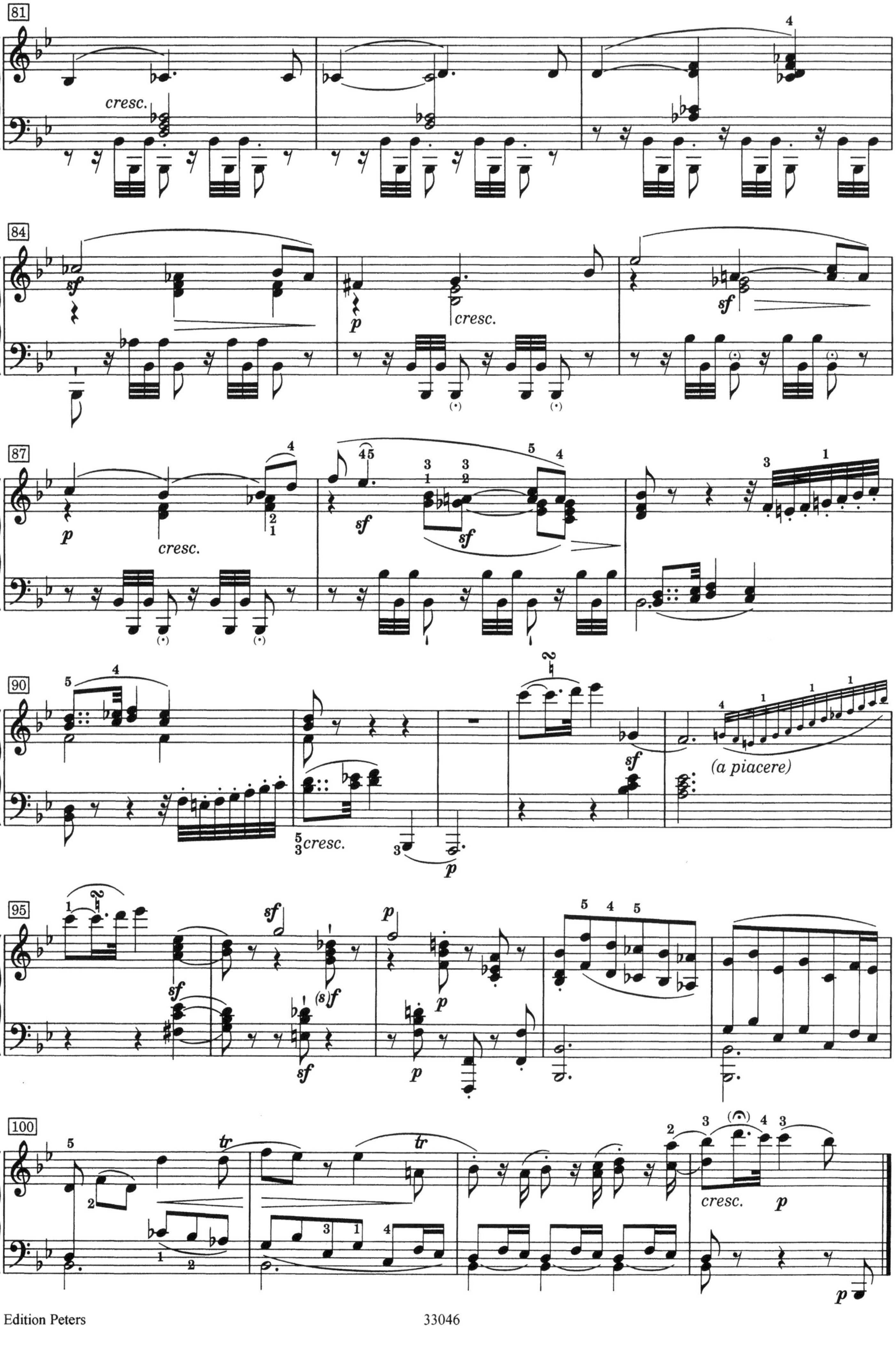
81
cresc.
84
sf
p
cresc.
sf
87
p
cresc.
sf
sf
90
cresc.
p
sf
(a piacere)
95
sf
sf
p
(s)f
sf
p
p
100
tr
tr
cresc.
p
p

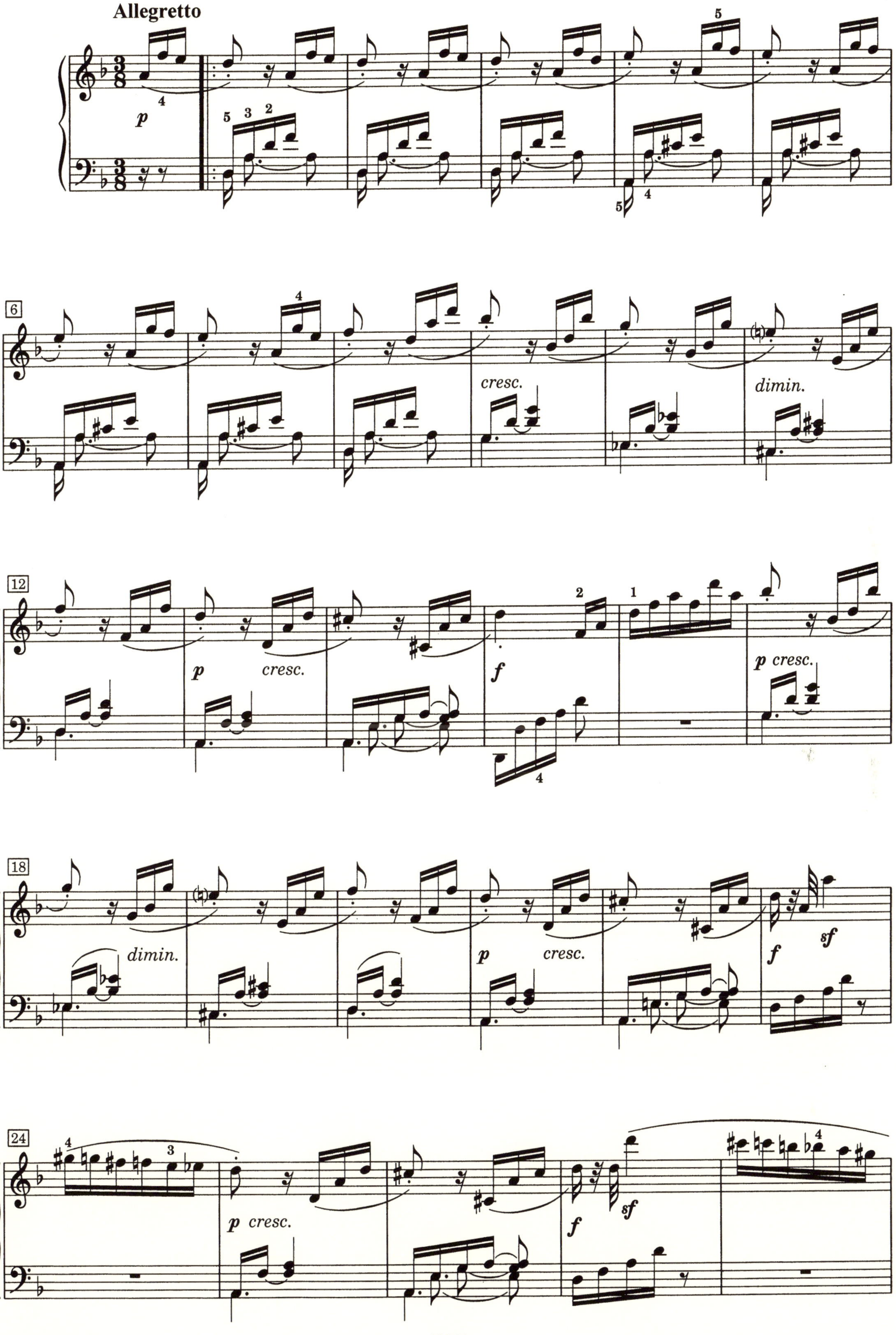
Allegretto
p
cresc.
dimin.
p cresc.
f
p cresc.
dimin.
p cresc.
f sf
p cresc.
f sf

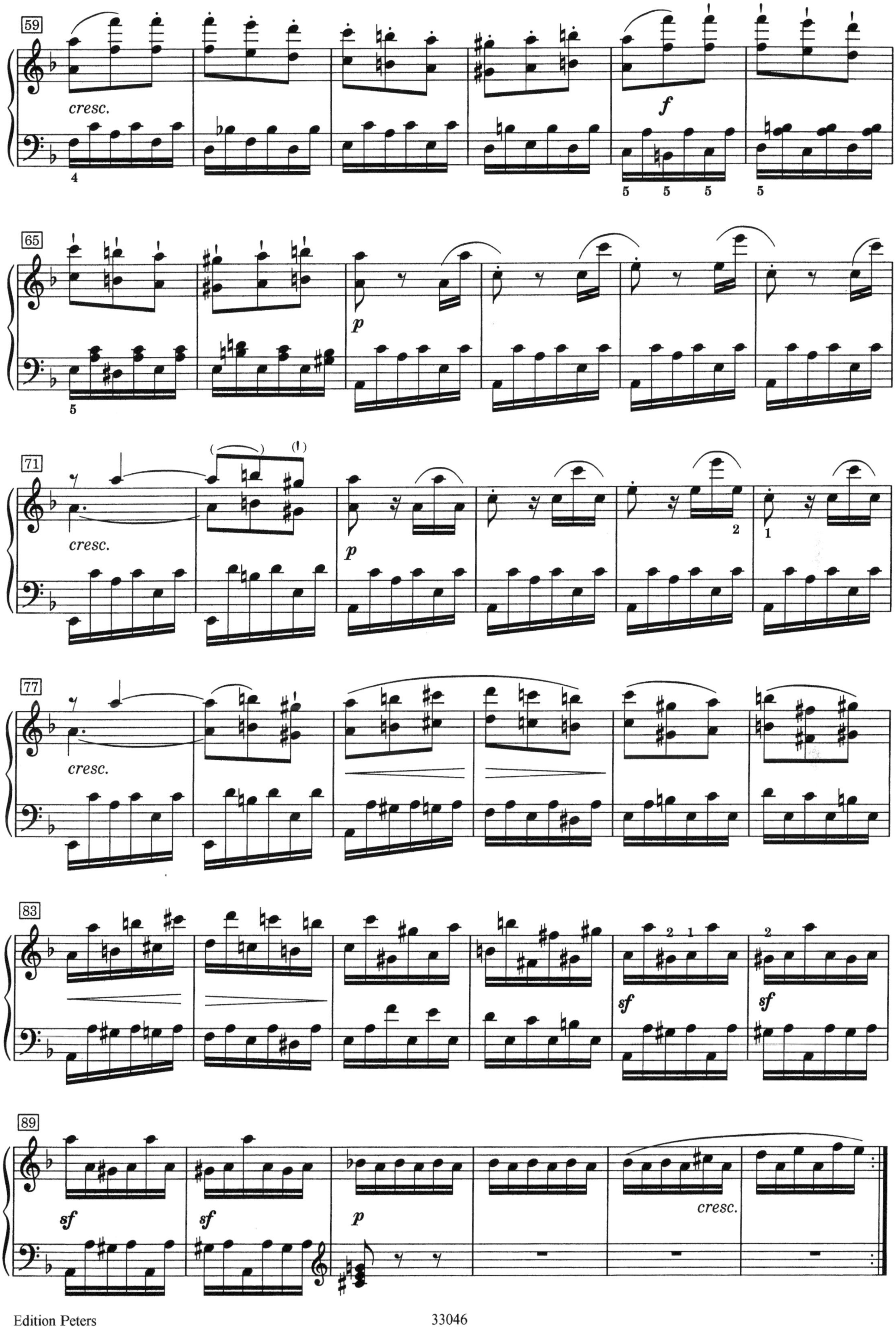
59
cresc.
f
65
p
71
cresc.
p
77
cresc.
83
sf
89
sf
sf
p
cresc.

*) Zur Lesart siehe Revisionsbericht.

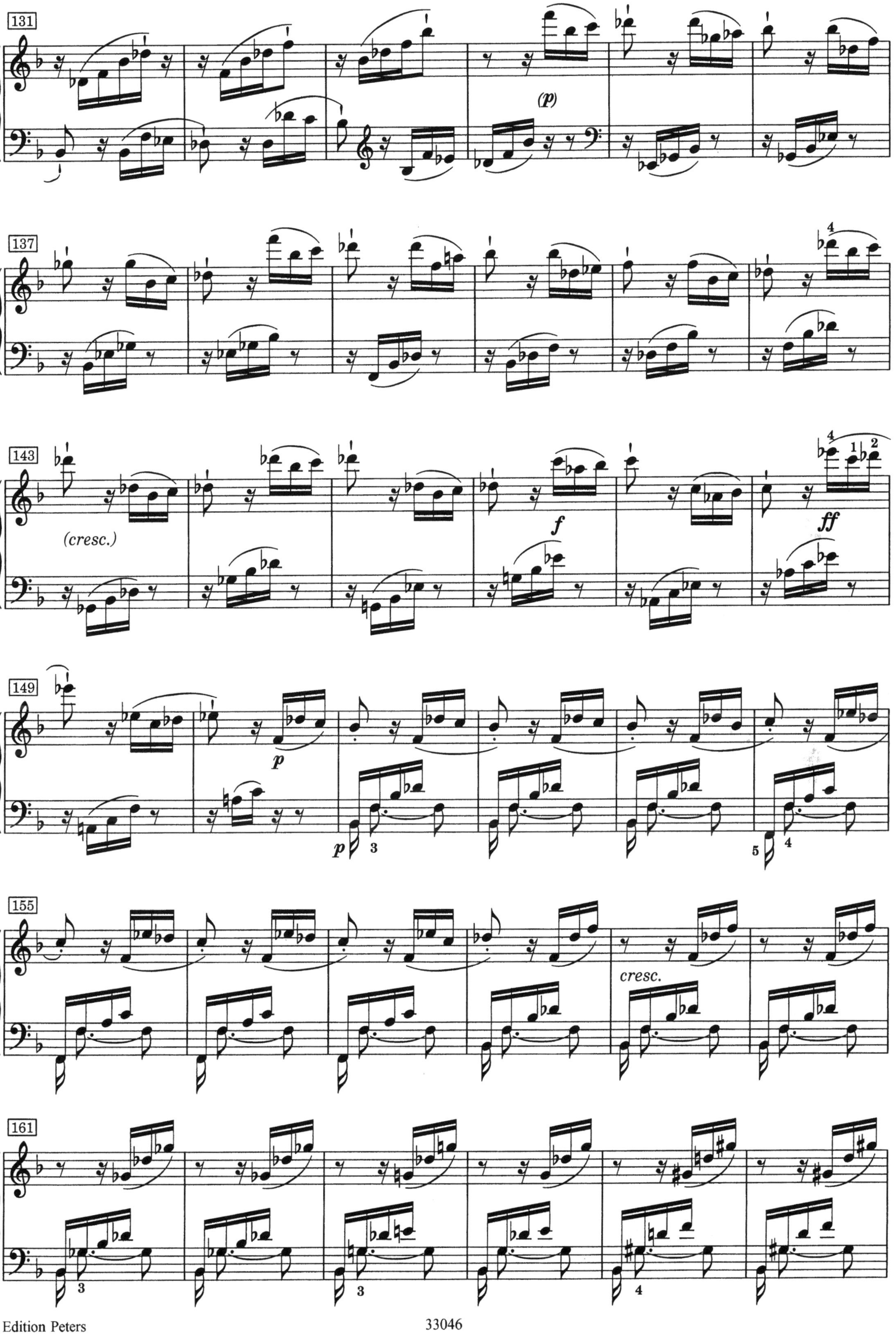
131
(p)
137
143
(cresc.)
f
ff
149
p
p
155
cresc.
161

*) Zur Lesart siehe Revisionsbericht.

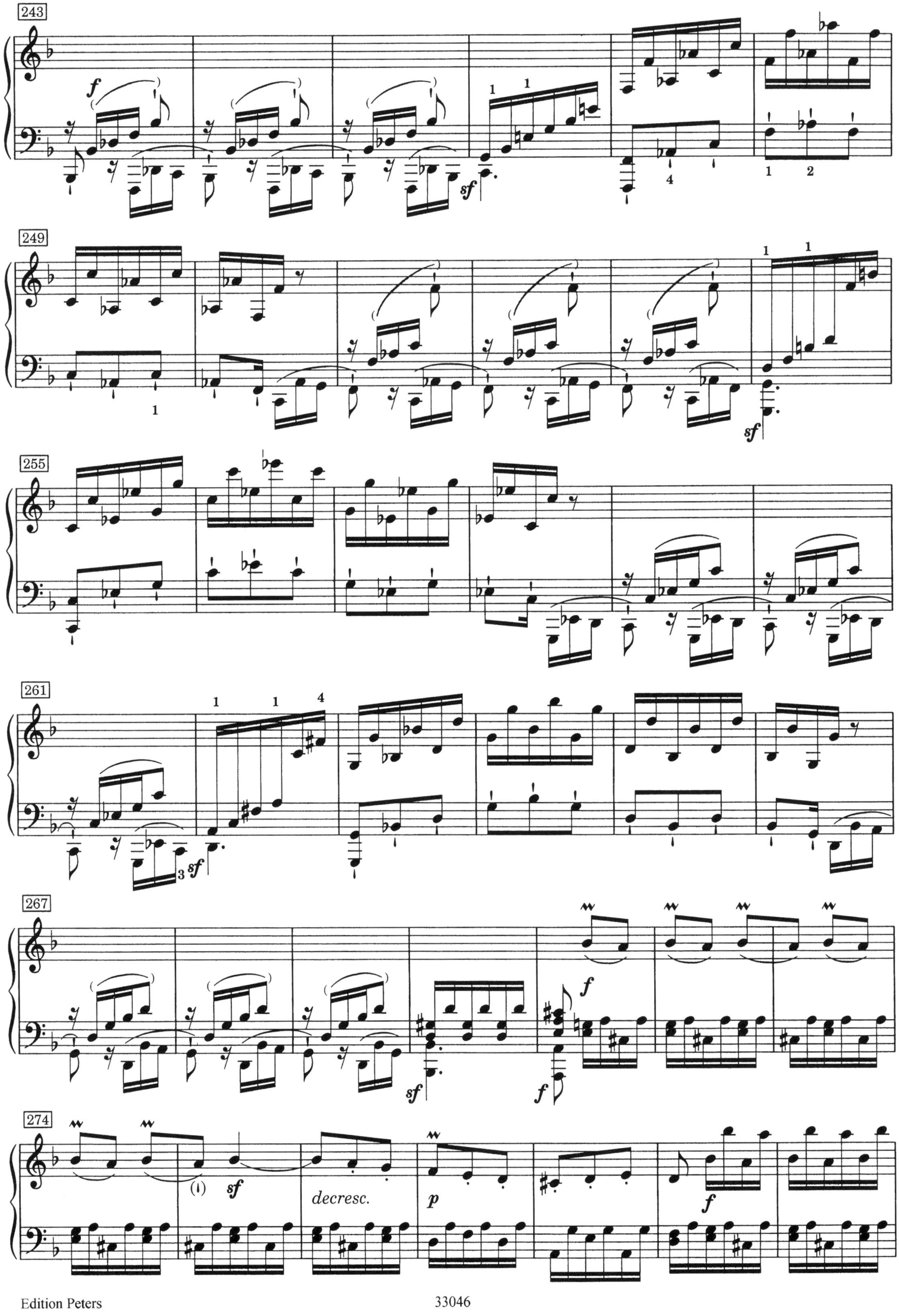
243
f
sf
249
sf
255
261
sf
267
sf
f
f
274
sf
decresc.
p
f

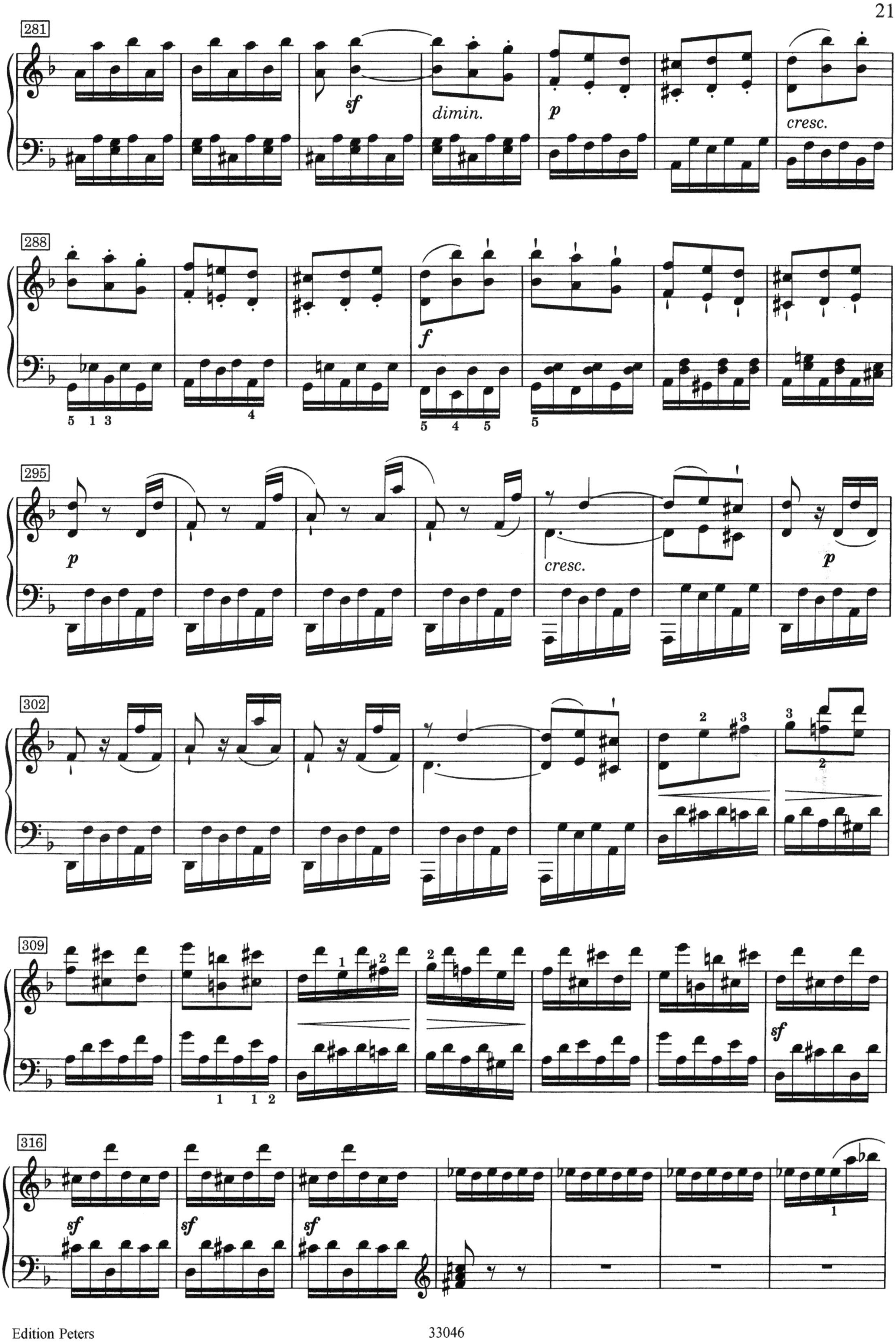
281
sf
dimin.
p
cresc.
288
f
295
p
cresc.
p
302
309
sf
316
sf
sf
sf

*) Zur Lesart siehe Revisionsbericht.

KOMMENTAR

Die Sonaten op. 31 Nr. 1–3 werden in Zürich von Hans Georg Nägeli in 2 Folgen herausgegeben. Den ersten Band stellt Nägeli in Leipzig anlässlich der Ostermesse 1803 vor:

DEUX / SONATES / Pour Le Piano Forte / Composées par / Louis van Beethoven / 5. Suite du Répertoire des Clavecinistes Prix 8"/ À Zuric chez Jean George Naigueli.

Darüber berichtet die *Allgemeine Musikalische Zeitung*:[1]

„*Bemerkungen über die so eben beendigte leipziger Ostermesse, in Hinsicht auf Musik.*
... eines der erschienenen Hefte enthält zwey, hier zuerst bekannt gemachte Sonaten von Beethoven, deren zweyte besonders dieses Künstlers eigene Art und Kunst sehr schön darlegt."

Erstmals veröffentlicht Beethoven Klaviersonaten ohne Widmung (und ohne Opuszahl). Die Uraufführung der Sonate op. 31 Nr. 2 findet in Wien statt, im Haus des Grafen Johann Georg Browne. Ferdinand Ries (1784–1838) erinnert sich an den denkwürdigen Abend (*Biographische Notizen über Beethoven*, 1838):[2]

„*... Eines Abends sollte ich beim Grafen Browne eine Sonate von Beethoven (A moll, Opus 23) spielen... Später mußte Beethoven spielen und wählte die D moll Sonate (Opus 31), welche eben erst erschienen war... und ich blätterte um. Bei dem Tacte 53 in 54 verfehlte Beethoven den Anfang und anstatt mit 2 und 2 Noten herunter zu gehen, schlug er mit der vollen Hand jedes Viertel (3 - 4 Noten zugleich) im Heruntergehen an. Es lautete, als sollte ein Clavier ausgeputzt werden. – Die Fürstinn gab ihm einige, nicht gar sanfte Schläge auf den Kopf, mit der Aeußerung: ‚Wenn der Schüler einen Finger für eine verfehlte Note erhält, so muß der Meister bei größeren Fehlern mit vollen Händen bestraft werden.' Alles lachte und Beethoven zuerst. Er fing nun aufs Neue an und spielte wunderschön, besonders trug er das Adagio unnachahmlich vor.*"

Die Erzählung verrät interessante Einzelheiten:
– Der Komponist selbst spielt die Uraufführung der Sonate op. 31 Nr. 2. Er spielt vom Blatt und benützt die Züricher Erstausgabe.
– Das Konzert findet im Frühjahr 1803 statt.
– Die „Fürstinn", von Ries auch „Fürstinn L............" genannt, Josephine von Liechtenstein, pflegt einen kameradschaftlichen Umgang mit Beethoven. (Er widmete ihr seine *Sonata quasi una Fantasia* Es-Dur op. 27 Nr. 1.)
– Merkwürdigerweise erwähnt Ries nicht das Finale der Sonate.

*

Das Konzept zur d-Moll-Sonate notierte Beethoven in einem „theatralischen", genauer „pantomimischen" Umfeld von Skizzen zur *Marcia funebre* für die Sonate As-Dur op. 26 und

COMMENTARY

The Sonatas op. 31 no. 1–3 were published in Zurich, Switzerland, by Hans Georg Nägeli, in two volumes. Nägeli presented the first volume in Leipzig, during the 1803 Easter Fair:

DEUX / SONATES / Pour Le Piano Forte / Composées par / Louis van Beethoven / 5. Suite du Répertoire des Clavecinistes Prix 8" / À Zuric chez Jean George Naigueli.

The *Allgemeine Musikalische Zeitung* reported:[1]

"*Remarks on the just ended Leipzig Easter Fair, with regard to musical events:*
... one of the volumes contains two, here for the first time acknowledged Sonatas from Beethoven, whereby the second one of them displays very nicely this artist's style and artistic virtue."

For the first time Beethoven published Piano Sonatas without a dedication (and without opus-number). The première of the Sonata op. 31 no. 2 took place in Vienna, at the residence of Count Johann Georg Browne. Ferdinand Ries (1784–1838) recalls that famous evening (*Biographische Notizen über Beethoven*, 1838):[2]

"*... One evening at Count Browne's I was to play a Beethoven Sonata (A minor, Opus 23)... Later that evening Beethoven was also obliged to play and chose the D minor Sonata (Opus 31), which had just been published. The Princess, who probably expected that Beethoven too would make a mistake somewhere, now stood behind his chair while I turned the pages. In bars 53 to 54 Beethoven missed the entry, and instead of descending two notes and then two more, he struck each quarter note in the descending passage with his whole hand (three or four notes at once). It sounded as if the piano was being cleaned. The Princess tapped him several times on the head, not at all delicately, saying: 'If the pupil receives one tap of the finger for one missed note, then the master must be punished with a full hand for worse mistakes.' Everyone laughed, Beethoven most of all. He started again and performed marvelously. The Adagio in particular was incomparably played.*"

The narrative reveals some interesting details:
– The composer himself played the première of the Sonata op. 31 no. 2. He played from the Zurich First Edition.
– The concert took place in the spring of 1803.
– The Princess, referred to by Ries as "Princess L............", Josephine von Liechtenstein, fostered a camaraderie-like conduct with Beethoven. (He dedicated to her his *Sonata quasi una Fantasia* in E♭ major op. 27 no. 1)
– Strangely enough, Ries does not mention any performance of the last movement.

*

The concept for the D minor Sonata Beethoven apostrophed between the "theatrical", or better "pantomimic" surrounding of sketches for the *Marcia funebre* of the Sonata A♭ major op. 26

---

[1] AMZ Nr. 35, Sp. 577 – 580, Leipzig, Mai 1803.
[2] Franz Gerhard Wegeler und Ferdinand Ries, *Biographische Notizen über Beethoven*.

[1] AMZ no. 35, column 577 – 580, Leipzig, May 1803.
[2] Franz Gerhard Wegeler and Ferdinand Ries, *Beethoven Remembered*, Arlington, Virginia, 1987.

and sketches for *Die Geschöpfe des Prometheus* op. 43 (sketchbook *Landsberg 7*, about 1800). We are to read keywords:[3]

"... *una Scena stromentale... Recitativ etc.... senza sord(ini)... D minor... Arioso... etc.... with feeling... molto allegro tutti*".

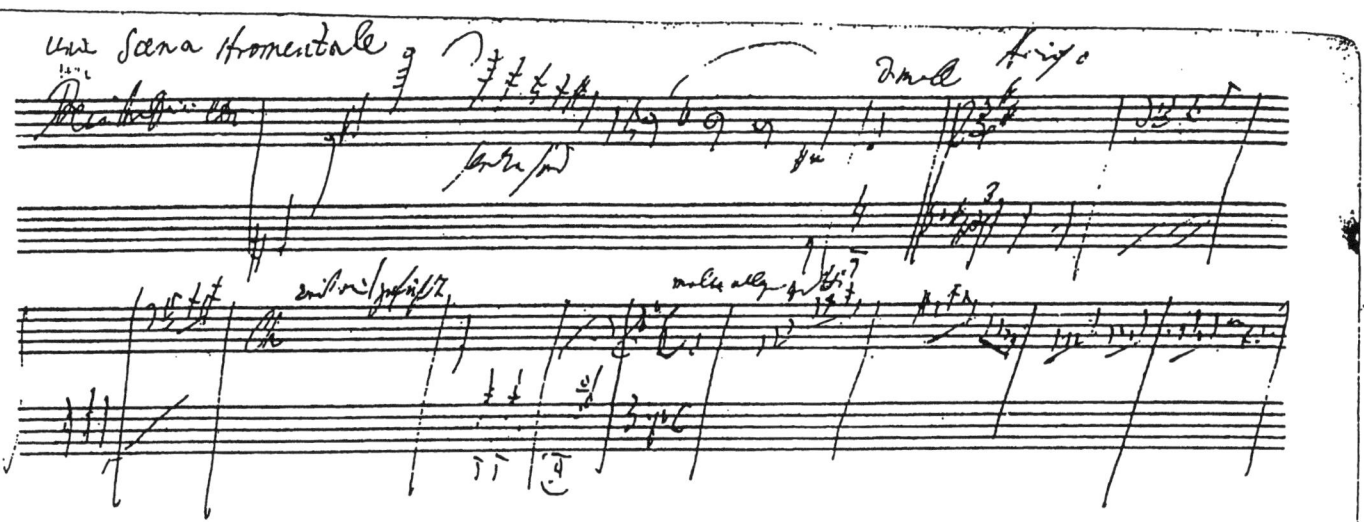

Ludwig van Beethoven, Skizzenbuch *Landsberg 7*, S. 134. Staatsbibliothek zu Berlin, Preußischer Kulturbesitz, Musikabteilung mit Mendelssohn-Archiv.

The first terms were elaborated in due time:

Scena (scene, stage, scenery) combined with the word *stromentale*, could mean "a scene for instrument(s)". This context leads one to believe, that Beethoven wanted his musical phantasies to stage-manage, in that case with the collaboration of the Pianoforte.

"*Recitativ etc.*" With the italian opera's *Recitativo secco* he formed the center of the first movement. He took the arpeggio chord and distributed it right to the beginning. Not enough, he forced it into the *alla breve* metre and confronted it with the soprano lament in the measures 21–28; it was to become the substance of the transition and of the development. All these manipulations the listener may experience as passing apparitions, as a *scenery*.

"*Senza sordini*" (without dampers, the dampers are raised = "𝒫"). To write an instruction for the pedal in that early point of planning is very surprising, but is to be appreciated as a compositional vision. The pedal offers a never dreamed of sound in the recitatives, which is intensified beyond endurance from measure 153 on by the blend of the C major arpeggio with the intonation on D♭. This effect conjures the echo of vaults, making a person insecure as to the direction of the course. Hopefully, after the fermata measure 158, the F minor is awaited. There, with dry, hollow beats, the dominant of F♯ minor sounds from the very depths. The listener is deprived of the orientation and welcomes any support.

"*D moll*", from measure 219 on. The last 10 measures emphasize the tonality of the movement, lending the listener an assuring foothold. The elaborate draft for the first movement in the *Keßler* sketchbook (1801–1802) surprisingly ends in D major.

---

[3] Not identified in Mikulicz, Schmidt, Johnson.

Beethovens Umgang mit dem Pedal trifft auch auf Unverständnis. Die Anhänger Johann Nepomuk Hummels (1778–1837), Komponist und brillanter Pianist,

„… warfen dem Beethoven vor, daß er das Fortepiano malträtiere, daß ihm alle Reinheit und Deutlichkeit mangle, daß er durch den Gebrauch des Pedals nur konfusen Lärm hervorbringe." – berichtet Carl Czerny (1791–1857).[4] Zum Pedal in Hummels Kompositionen meint Czerny:

„In Hummels Werken findet man es selten, und kann es auch meistens entbehren."[5]

Der 2. Satz *Adagio* wird mit einem „neutralen" Arpeggio eingeleitet. Damit ist der Bezug zu den Rezitativen im 1. Satz hergestellt. Dann beginnt ein nachdenklicher Monolog, der zunehmend dem Muster des *Recitativo stromentato* gleicht. Sein Gegenstück ist die *dolce*-Melodie ab Takt 31. Zusätzlich verstärken Trommelschläge, im Diskant wiederholt, die orchestrale Struktur der Rezitative. Die Coda ist ausgesprochen versöhnlich.

Musste man Beethoven damals inständig bitten, auch den letzten Satz zu spielen? Wir können uns vorstellen, dass Beethoven hinreißend über die arpeggierten Akkorde fantasierte, sich in den beruhigenden Figuren der Rechten Hand verlor, um die Zuhörer temperamentvoll durch Forte-Eruptionen aufzuschrecken. Vielleicht unterstützte er gar, als Attraktion, die chromatischen Läufe mit Pedal, um dem Finale ein an das Cymbal erinnerndes, ungarisches Kolorit zu verleihen.

*

Nach vielen Jahrzehnten kommt Anton Schindler (1795–1864) in seiner Biographie Ludwig van Beethovens auf ein Konzert bei Carl Czerny zu sprechen:

„Eines Tages, als ich dem Meister den tiefen Eindruck geschildert, den die Sonaten in D moll und F moll (Op. 31 und 57) in der Versammlung bei C. Czerny hervorgebracht und er in guter Stimmung war, bat ich ihn, mir den Schlüssel zu diesen Sonaten zu geben. Er erwiderte: ‚Lesen Sie nur Shakespeare's Sturm.' Dort also sollte er zu finden seyn; aber an welcher Stelle? Frager, lese, rathe und errathe!"

Wilhelm von Lenz greift diesen Gedanken auf und meint:[6]

„Die spekulative Kritik hat anzunehmen, daß weder die eine noch die andere (Sonate) den S t u r m zum Libretto (Programm) hat, sondern nur das phantastische Element jener unvergleichlichen dramatischen Phantasie im Allgemeinen in den Sonaten Anwendung auf einen Instrumentaltext findet."

Er kann dennoch der Versuchung nicht widerstehen, einzelne Szenen des Dramas der d-Moll-Sonate gegenüber zu stellen. Damit hat sich für op. 31 Nr. 2 der Untertitel „Sturmsonate" eingebürgert.

*

Die vorliegende Neuausgabe beruht auf der Erstausgabe von Hans Georg Nägeli, Zürich, und den Nachdrucken von Nikolaus Simrock, Bonn, und Jean (Johann) Cappi, Wien. Das Manuskript ist verschollen. F. Ries schreibt, dass Beethoven

---

[4] Friedrich Kerst, *Die Erinnerungen an Beethoven*.
[5] Carl Czerny, *Von dem Vortrage*.
[6] W. v. Lenz, *Kritischer Katalog sämmtlicher Werke Ludwig van Beethovens*.

Beethoven's use of the pedal was met with ignorance, too. The devotees of Johann Nepomuk Hummel (1778–1837), composer and brilliant pianist himself,

"…accused Beethoven of maltreating the pianoforte, missing any purity and discretion and creating by his use of the pedal only a confusing noise." – remembered Carl Czerny (1791–1857).[4] As regards the pedal in Hummel's compositions, Czerny meant:

"In the works of Hummel one finds it seldom, and mostly one can do without."[5]

The second movement *Adagio* starts with a "neutral" arpeggio, acting as a bridge to the recitatives in the first movement. Then a meditative monologue begins, which gradually equals the model of the *Recitativo stromentato*. Its counterpart is the *dolce* melody from measure 31 on. A percussive effect, repeated in the treble, supports the orchestral structure of the recitatives. The Coda is outspoken placating.

Was Beethoven to be begged for the last movement, at Count Browne's residence? We are tempted to believe that Beethoven fantasized on the arpeggiated chords in a ravishing manner. Temperamental as he was, he lost himself in the tranquilizing figures of the Right Hand, only to surprise the auditory with Forte eruptions. Perhaps, as an attraction, he blended the chromatic scales with the pedal, cymbal-like, giving the Finale a hungarian color.

*

Many decades later Anton Schindler (1795–1864), in his Biography on Ludwig van Beethoven, mentioned a recital at Carl Czerny's studio:

"One day, when I informed the master of the deep impression which the Sonatas in D minor and in F minor (Op. 31 and 57) aroused at C. Czerny's gathering, he was in a good mood. So I asked him for an explanatory advice on these Sonatas. He answered: 'Do read Shakespeare's Tempest.' There it should be found; but where? Questioner, read, guess and solve!"

Wilhelm von Lenz, prompted by this train of thoughts, commented:[6]

"The speculative review has to assume that neither the one (Sonata) nor the other is depending on the contents of T h e T e m p e s t, that on the contrary only the phantastic element in that incomparable dramatic fantasie, generally spoken, is introduced into those Sonatas."

However, *von Lenz* could not restrain himself from comparing particular scenes in Shakespeare's drama with the D minor Sonata. From there on, the subtitle "The Tempest" for op. 31 no. 2 was established.

*

This new edition depends on Hans Georg Nägeli's First Edition and the reprints by Nikolaus Simrock, Bonn, and by Jean (Johann) Cappi, Vienna. The manuscript is lost. F. Ries reported, that Beethoven was very angered with the printed

---

[4] Friedrich Kerst, *Die Erinnerungen an Beethoven*.
[5] Carl Czerny, *Von dem Vortrage*.
[6] W. v. Lenz, *Kritischer Katalog sämmtlicher Werke Ludwig van Beethovens*.

über den Züricher Notentext der G-Dur-Sonate op. 31 Nr. 1 höchst aufgebracht war. Hatte Nägeli versehentlich eine frühe Fassung (Urfassung) der 1. Sonate erhalten? Da er die Zusendung von Korrektur-Abzügen unterlassen hatte, konnte Beethoven einer Neuausgabe der Sonaten (zunächst Nr. 1 und Nr. 2) bei Simrock zustimmen. Die Korrekturen besorgt Ries. Diese „*Edition très correcte, Oeuvre 31*" erscheint im August 1803.[7] Eine Besonderheit der Ausgabe Simrock ist der beharrliche Einsatz des Bassschlüssels für die Rechte Hand, sobald diese tiefe Passagen spielt.

Im folgenden Jahr[8] druckt Cappi die Sonaten Nr. 1 und Nr. 2, als „*Oeuvre 29*"[9]. Das Notenbild ist der Züricher Vorlage sehr ähnlich, aber der Text wurde von Beethoven korrigiert. Aus gutem Grund zeigt Cappi diese Ausgabe nicht an.

Einzelheiten zu den Ausgaben bringt der Revisionsbericht.

Die Zeichen für das Staccato korrespondieren mit Beethovens Manuskripten: • = leichtes Staccato; ׀ = etwas aggressives Staccato (*cresc.→f*).[10]

Fingersätze sind häufig der individuellen Interpretation unterworfen. Deshalb sind die Fingersätze des Herausgebers als Anregung zu verstehen. Beethovens Fingersätze im 3. Satz sind *kursiv* gedruckt. Die Vorschläge des Herausgebers stehen in runden Klammern.

Der Herausgeber dankt der Staatsbibliothek zu Berlin, Preußischer Kulturbesitz, Musikabteilung mit Mendelssohn-Archiv, für die Kopie der Eintragung im Skizzenbuch *Landsberg 7*; sowie den im Revisionsbericht genannten Bibliotheken für die Überlassung von Kopien der Erstausgabe und der Nachdrucke. Kurt Dorfmüller gab wertvolle Hinweise auf das Datum der Ausgabe Simrock und zum Standort der 1. Titelauflage der Ausgabe Cappi; ihm sei herzlich gedankt. Der Österreichischen Nationalbibliothek Wien, Digitaler Bildservice, insbesondere Frau Katrin Ferschitz, gilt großer Dank für die gewährte Einsicht in die wertvollen Bände der *Wiener Zeitung*.

Der Herausgeber dankt John W. Maerhofer, Professor emeritus, Chair Fine Arts and Humanities, College of Southern Maryland, USA, für die hilfreichen Korrekturen in der englischen Übersetzung.

Mai/May 2010

version of the G major Sonata op. 31 no. 1 in the Zurich Edition. Had Nägeli received erroneously an early version (Urfassung) of the 1st Sonata? Since he did not deliver the customary proof sheets, Beethoven was in a position to agree to a new edition of the Sonatas by Simrock (at first nos. 1 and 2). Ries was to pass on the corrections. This "*Edition très correcte, Oeuvre 31*" was announced in August 1803.[7] A peculiarity of the Simrock edition is its permanent use of the bass-key for the Right Hand, as soon it reaches into deeper passages.

In the next year[8] Cappi printed the Sonatas no. 1 and no. 2, as "*Oeuvre 29*".[9] His print is astonishing by its narrow resemblance to the Zurich print, but the text is corrected by Beethoven. It is understandable, that Cappi did not announce his edition.

Details of the different editions are listed in the Revision Report.

The signs for the Staccato used in this edition relate to Beethoven's different signs in his manuscripts: • is a light Staccato; ׀ is a somewhat aggressive Staccato (*cresc.→f*).[10]

The fingering often depends on the individual musical interpretation. Therefore the editor's fingering is to be understood as suggestion for one's own experience. Beethoven's authentic fingering in the third movement are printed in italics. Any recommandations from the editor are in round parenthesis.

The editor would like to thank the Staatsbibliothek zu Berlin, Preußischer Kulturbesitz, Musikabteilung mit Mendelssohn-Archiv, for the copy of the entry in the sketchbook *Landsberg 7*. Additional thanks are extended to the archives and collections as named in the Revision Report for providing copies from the First Edition and the reprints of op. 31. Kurt Dorfmüller is thanked for his valuable information about the date of Simrock's edition, and about the library, which keeps the 1st Title Edition of Cappi's print. The editor is grateful to the Österreichische Nationalbibliothek and to Mrs. Katrin Ferschitz, Digital Services, for the granted use of the precious volumes of the *Wiener Zeitung*.

The editor is indebted to John W. Maerhofer, Professor emeritus, Chair Fine Arts and Humanities, The College of Southern Maryland, USA, for his valuable contributions to the English translation.

Johannes Fischer

---

[7] *Kaiserlich-privilegirter Reichs=Anzeiger. Num. 224. Sp. 2922. Mittwochs, den 24. August 1803.*

[8] Georg Kinsky und Hans Halm, *Das Werk Beethovens*, geben für den Cappi-Nachdruck das Jahr 1803 an. Das scheint, nach dem Vergleich der Platten-Nummern mit der Annoncen Cappis für andere Werke in der *Wiener Zeitung* (*Alexander Weinmann*), zu früh angesetzt.

[9] Die Opuszahl 29 war bereits für das Streichquintett C-Dur vergeben.

[10] Johannes Fischer, *Das Staccato in L. v. Beethovens Klaviersonaten.*

---

[7] *Kaiserlich-privilegirter Reichs=Anzeiger. Num. 224. column 2922. Mittwochs, den 24. August 1803.*

[8] Georg Kinsky and Hans Halm, *Das Werk Beethovens*, suggest the year 1803 for Cappi's print. With regard to the plate numbers and announcements of other editions by Cappi (*Alexander Weinmann*) in the *Wiener Zeitung*, 1803 seems to be too early.

[9] The opus number 29 belongs already to the String Quintet in C major.

[10] Johannes Fischer, *Das Staccato in L. v. Beethovens Klaviersonaten.*

REVISIONSBERICHT

EA Erstausgabe
NA Neue Ausgabe
N EA Nägeli, Zürich 1803
S NA Simrock, Bonn
C NA Cappi, Wien
O.S. Oberes Notensystem. U.S. Unteres Notensystem
R.H. Rechte Hand (*mano destra, m.d.*)
L.H. Linke Hand (*mano sinistra, m.s.*)

Skizzen:
Notierungsbuch *Landsberg 7*, S. 134. Staatsbibliothek zu Berlin, Preußischer Kulturbesitz, Musikabteilung mit Mendelssohn-Archiv. Übertragen von Karl Lothar Mikulicz.
Skizzenbuch *Keßler*. Archiv der Gesellschaft der Musikfreunde Wien. Übertragen von Sieghard Brandenburg.
Manuskript: verschollen.
Erstausgabe: („Urfassung"?). Zürich, Frühjahr 1803. Anzeige des Erscheinens: AMZ Nr. 35, Sp. 577 – 580, Leipzig, Mai 1803. Vorgelegt zur Leipziger Ostermesse 1803.
DEUX / SONATES / Pour Le Piano Forte / Composées par / Louis van Beethoven / 5.* Suite du Répertoire des Clavecinistes – Prix 8". / À Zuric chez Jean George Naigueli. (Zusammen mit op. 31 Nr. 1). Innentitel: *SONATA I.* und *SONATA II.* *Die Zahl ist handschriftlich. Platten-Nr. *5*.[11]
Keine Widmung, keine Opus-Zahl, Bayerische Staatsbibliothek München, Musiksammlung. Österreichische Nationalbibliothek Wien, Musiksammlung.
Neue Ausgabe: Bonn, August 1803, angekündigt im „*Kaiserlich privilegirten Reichs=Anzeiger Num. 224. Mittwochs, den 24. August 1803*". (Sp. 2922) „Revision".
Deux Sonates, / pour le Piano-forte, / Composeés par / Louis van Beethoven. / Œuvre 31* / Editiou tres Correcte. / Prix 6 francs. / À Bonn, chez N. Simrock. / À PARIS chez H. Simrock, professeur, marchand de musique et d'instrumens, rue du Mont.blanc № 373, / chaussée d'Antin au coin de celle basse du rempart. Platten-Nr. *345*. (Zusammen mit op. 31 Nr. 1). Innentitel: *SONATA / I.* und *SONATA / II.* *Die Zahl ist handschriftlich. Bayerische Staatsbibliothek München, Musiksammlung.
Neue Ausgabe: Wien, 1804. Die Zeitangabe „1803" (Kinsky/ Halm) scheint verfrüht. Siehe Fußnote im Kommentar.
Deux / SONATES / pour le Clavecin ou Piano – Forte / composées / par / LOUIS van BEETHOVEN / Œuvre 29. № 2.* / à Vienne chez Jean Cappi, / Place S'. Michel № 5./
Verlags-und Platten-Nr: *1027.1028*. Innentitel: *SONATA. / I* und *SONATA. / II.* *Die Zahl ist handschriftlich. Bayerische Staatsbibliothek München, Musiksammlung. Bibliothek der Hochschule für Musik Ferenc Liszt, Budapest.
1. Titelauflage Cappi: Vor dem 3. Mai 1806.[12]
Trois / SONATES /... mit gleicher Adresse (*Place S'. Michel № 5*), mit drei Verlags-Nummern auf dem Titelblatt: *1027.1028.1115*. Einzelausgabe mit der Platten-Nr. *1028*. Kumitachi College, Music Library, Tokyo, Japan.
2. Titelauflage Cappi: Nach dem 3. Mai 1806. Neue Adresse: *Place S'. Michel № 4.* Archiv der Gesellschaft der Musikfreunde Wien, aus der Sammlung des Erzherzogs Rudolph von Österreich. Handschriftliche Eintragungen.

---

[11] Identifiziert von Norbert Gertsch und Murray Perahia, in: *Ludwig van Beethoven, Klaviersonate Nr. 17 d-moll Opus 31 Nr. 2.*
[12] Adreßänderungs-Anzeige des Verlages Cappi in der *Wiener Zeitung* Nr. 36 vom 3. Mai 1806.

Largo – Allegro

T. 1,7,93,95,97,143,153, R.H. 3. und 4. Viertel: Portato-Bögen in S, wohl Korrektur von F. Ries; nicht in N und C. Das freie Hinzufügen der Töne über dem Grundakkord gerät durch den Portato-Bogen in eine zeitabhängige Bewegung. Spätere Ausgaben folgen S.
T. 6 Fermate nach S und C.
T. 55 kein Staccato in den Quellen. Neuere Ausgaben gleichen an T. 185 an.
T. 68 L.H. kein Legato-Bogen in den Quellen. Neuere Ausgaben gleichen an T. 198 an.
T. 69 L.H. kein *p* in den Quellen. R.H. kein *p* in C. Neuere Ausgaben gleichen an T. 199 an.
T. 75 kein *p* in den Quellen. Neuere Ausgaben gleichen an T. 205 an.
T. 75-76 L.H. Haltebogen *e-e* in S. (T. 205-206 L.H. Haltebogen *A-A* in C.)
T. 89^1/ 90^1 Haltebögen nach S.
T. 107 kein *f* in den Quellen. Neuere Ausgaben gleichen an T. 29 an.
T. 119 R.H. Oktave *gis'-gis"* Staccato in S.
T. 143 Largo. Kein *pp* in den Quellen. Arpeggio in S. Kein Arpeggio in N und C, weil dieses in T. 137 durch die Vorschlagsnoten antizipiert wird.
T. 152 *adagio* Kein Legato-Bogen für die R.H., keine ===== - Gabel in N und C. S gleicht an die Exposition an.
T. 153ff. Handschriftliche Eintragungen in einem Exemplar der 2. Titelauflage Cappi, Wien, ehemalige Musiksammlung des Erzherzogs Rudolph von Österreich: T. 153 Portato *e'-g'*; T. 155 Sechzehntel *des'→c'*; T. 156 Haltebogen *b-b*. Gedruckt wird der Haltebogen erstmals in der Ausgabe Haslinger, Wien, und daraufhin von neueren Ausgaben. Ein Unterrichts-Gespräch zwischen Beethoven und dem Erzherzog?
T. 168,169 Der verminderte Septakkord *gis-h-d'-f'* (Ries' Korrektur?) steht in S in T. 170.

T. 170 Der Pianist Johannes Pawlica, München, betont den kadenzartigen Charakter der Passage mit einer Fermate.
T. 175 R.H. Staccato nach C.
T. 179 R.H. Staccato nach N und C.
T. 185-193 Die Artikulation unterscheidet sich in den Quellen von der Artikulation in der Exposition.
T. 199 L.H. *p* nach N und C. Nicht in S.
T. 204-205 R.H. kein Legato-Bogen *cis"- d"* in den Quellen, siehe aber T. 74-75.
T. 205 *p* nach den Quellen.
T. 205-206 L.H. Haltebogen *A-A* in C.
T. 215-217 L.H. Legato-Bogen in S.

Adagio

T. 1 kurzes Arpeggio.
T. 5 Die Koloratur ist frei und ohne Taktmaß zu spielen.
T. 10 und folgende, Ausführung nach Artur Schnabel:

T. 17 R.H. Staccato in S.
T. 23 R.H. 1. Viertel kein *p* in den Quellen. Neuere Ausgaben gleichen an T. 65 an.
T. 27 *p* nicht in C.
T. 30, 72 L.H. 1. Achtel kein Staccato in den Quellen.
T. 42 L.H. 3. Achtel kein Staccato in den Quellen.
T. 49 Das crescendo bezieht sich, im Gegensatz zu T. 7, auf die L.H.
T. 56 L.H. 6. 32tel *es* in N und C, *f* in S.
T. 57, 58 R.H. 3. Viertel kein Staccato in den Quellen.
T. 76 R.H. 1. Viertel: Rhythmus nach den Quellen. Siehe aber T. 34.
T. 77 L.H. 3. Achtel nur *d'* in N, keine Terz *d'-f'*.
T. 99 Urfassung in N:

Revision in S und C.
T. 103 R.H. 6. Achtel keine Pause in N und C.

Allegretto

Die Artikulation ist in den Quellen keinesfalls stereotyp; Beethoven hält sein freies Spiel der Passagen fest.

T. 94 Lesart N:

T. 109-110 L.H. keine Haltebögen in den Quellen. Der Akkord T. 110 wird angeschlagen. Neuere Ausgaben binden über.
T. 127 L.H. ♭ vor *d* in S und C.
T. 146 *f* in N und S; nicht in C.
T. 173 *p* fehlt in S.
T.175-176; 183-184; 187-188 L.H. Legato-Bogen und Fingersatz (autograph) nach S und C.
T. 183 L.H. Mittelstimme *e'* (statt ♭*e'*) in N und C. *d'* in S.
T. 275 R.H. 1. Achtel kein Staccato in den Quellen.
T. 305 kein crescendo in den Quellen.
T. 319 kein *p* in den Quellen.
T. 334 R.H. 4. 16tel *f"* nach den Quellen. Neuere Ausgaben gleichen an und bringen *e"*.
T. 376 wohl irrtümlich *dim.* statt *cresc.* in den Quellen. (Dort Schreibweise stets *dimin.*)

Literatur/Literature

Georg Kinsky und Hans Halm, *Thematisch-Bibliographisches Verzeichnis aller vollendeten Werke Ludwig van Beethovens*, München 1955.
Wilhelm von Lenz, *Kritischer Katalog sämtlicher Werke Ludwig van Beethovens, Die D Moll-Sonate op. 31*, S. 169 ff. Zweite, verbesserte Auflage. Hamburg 1860.
Alexander Weinmann, *Beiträge zur Geschichte des Alt-Wiener Musikverlages, Verlagsverzeichnis Giovanni Cappi bis Adolf Othmar Witzendorf*, Wien 1967.
Allgemeine Musikalische Zeitung, AMZ Nr. 35, Sp. 577–580, Leipzig, Mai 1803. Bayerische Staatsbibliothek München, Musiksammlung.
Kaiserlich privilegirter Reichs=Anzeiger. Num. 224. Sp. 2922. Mittwochs, den 24. August 1803.
Franz Gerhard Wegeler und Ferdinand Ries, *Biographische Notizen über Beethoven*, S. 88–90 und S. 92–93. 2. Nachdruck der Ausgaben Koblenz 1838 und 1848, G. Olms, Hildesheim, Zürich, New York 2000.
—*Beethoven Remembered, The Biographical Notes of Franz Wegeler and Ferdinand Ries*, translated from the German by Frederick Noonan, S. 77–79, S. 81–82, Arlington, Virginia 1987.
Friedrich Kerst, *Die Erinnerungen an Beethoven*, Band I, daraus: *Carl Czernys Aufzeichnungen für Otto Jahn*, S. 44, Stuttgart 1913.
Ulrich Mahlert (Herausgeber), *Carl Czerny, Von dem Vortrage, Wien 1839*, S. 47, Faksimile-Ausgabe, Wiesbaden 1991.
Anton Schindler, *Biographie von Ludwig van Beethoven*, Zweiter Teil, S. 221. 5. Auflage, Münster 1927. Reprint der dritten Auflage, Münster 1860.
Gustav Nottebohm, *Zweite Beethoveniana, Ein Skizzenbuch aus dem Jahre 1800*, Leipzig 1887.
Karl Lothar Mikulicz, *Ein Notierungsbuch von Ludwig van Beethoven*, Leipzig 1927 („Landsberg 7").
Hans Schmidt, *Verzeichnis der Skizzen Beethovens*, Beethoven-Jahrbuch Jahrgang 1965/68, Beethovenhaus Bonn 1969.
Douglas Johnson, Alan Tyson & Robert Winter, *The Beethoven Sketchbooks*, Oxford 1985.
Ludwig van Beethoven, *Keßlersches Skizzenbuch*, Publikationen der Sammlungen der Gesellschaft der Musikfreunde in Wien, herausgegeben von Otto Biba, mit einem Nachwort und einem Register von Sieghard Brandenburg, München-Salzburg, o.J. Übertragung in: Sieghard Brandenburg, *Keßlersches Skizzenbuch*, Veröffentlichungen des Beethovenhauses in Bonn, 1978.
Artur Schnabel, *Beethoven, 32 Sonate per Pianoforte, Volume secondo (13 a 23)*, Milano 1949.
Norbert Gertsch und Murray Perahia, *Ludwig van Beethoven, Klaviersonate Nr. 17 d-moll Opus 31 Nr. 2*, München 2003.
Johannes Fischer, *Vom Skizzenblatt zum Urtext. Ludwig van Beethovens „Edition très correcte"*, Mainz 1985.
—*Das Staccato in Ludwig van Beethovens Klaviersonaten*, in: Musikalische Aufführungspraxis und Edition, S. 151ff., Regensburg 1990.
—*Ludwig van Beethoven, Klaviersonate d-Moll op. 31 Nr.2 („Sturmsonate"), Neuausgabe mit Kommentar und Revisionsbericht*, 2004. Vergriffen.